TRON THEATRE COMPANY
presents

A SLOW AIR

by David Harrower

Premiered at the Tron Theatre from 11–21 May 2011
as part of the Mayfesto festival; then presented at
the Edinburgh Fringe from 5–21 August 2011.

A Slow Air
by David Harrower

Cast

Morna	Kathryn Howden
Athol	Lewis Howden

Creative Team

Director	David Harrower
Designer	Jessica Brettle
Composer	Daniel Padden
Lighting Designer	Dave Shea
Deputy Stage Manager	Suzie Goldberg
Student Placement	Sarah McComish
Scenic Artists	Neil Haynes
	Christine Orr

Tron Theatre Production Staff

Production Manager	Jo Masson
Technical Manager	Malcolm Rogan
Stage Manager	David Sneddon
Assistant Stage Manager for Mayfesto	Kieron Johnson
Chief LX	Mark Hughes
Head of Sound	Barry McCall
Technical Stage Manager	Karen Bryce
Production Photography	Richard Campbell
PR	Liz Smith

The performance lasts approximately 1 hour and 20 minutes

Biographies

David Harrower *Writer & Director*
David is an internationally acclaimed playwright. Previous theatre work includes: Knives in Hens, Dark Earth, Kill the Old Torture Their Young (Traverse Theatre), The Chrysalids (NT Connections), Presence (Royal Court), Blackbird (Edinburgh International Festival, West End, Manhattan Theatre Club, Sydney Theatre Company), 365 (National Theatre of Scotland). Adaptations include Büchner's Woyzeck (Edinburgh Lyceum), Ödön von Horváth's Tales from the Vienna Woods, Chekhov's Ivanov (National Theatre), Schiller's Mary Stuart (National Theatre of Scotland), Pirandello's Six Characters in Search of an Author, Schnitzler's Liebelei as Sweet Nothings, Brecht's The Good Soul of Szechuan, and Gogol's The Government Inspector (Young Vic).

Lewis Howden *Athol*
Trained at the RSAMD, Lewis has worked extensively in theatres throughout the UK and abroad. Tron productions include Defender of the Faith, The Beauty Queen of Leenane, The Trick is to Keep Breathing and The Witches of Pollock. Other recent theatre work includes: Educating Agnes, Confessions of a Justified Sinner, Tartuffe, Merlin the Magnificent, Mother Courage, Cuttin' a Rug, Changed Days (Royal Lyceum), Any Given Day, Petrol Jesus Nightmare, The Nest, Olga, Knives in Hens, Loose Ends, The House Among The Stars (Traverse Theatre), The Company Will Overlook A Moment Of Madness, A Dead Man's Dying (Òran Mór/NTS), Mary Queen of Scots Got Her Head Chopped Off, Our Teacher's a Troll (National Theatre of Scotland), Macbeth, Educating Agnes, Medea, King Lear (Theatre Babel), 27 Wagons Full Of Cotton, The Big Funk, The Crucible, Glengarry Glen Ross (The Arches), No Mean City, Nightingale and Chase (Citizens Theatre), Riddance (Paines Plough), Fire In The Basement (Communicado), Broken Glass, Frankie and Johnny (Rapture), Word for Mouth (Magnetic North), The Angel's Share (Borderline), Algebra Of Freedom (7.84) and Quelques Fleurs (Nippy Sweeties). Recent television work includes Hope Springs, Taggart, Monarch of the Glen, Rebus and Still Game. Film credits include The Boxer, Slide Aberdeen, The Blue Boy and Gare Au Male.

Kathryn Howden *Morna*
Tron productions include: That Face, Tartuffe and Shining Souls. Recent theatre productions include: The Last Witch (Edinburgh International Festival/Traverse Theatre), The Ballad of Crazy Paola, Abandonment, Passing Places, Poor Superman (co-produced with Hampstead Theatre), Any Given Day, The Hope Slide and Buchanan (Traverse Theatre), Be Near Me (National Theatre of Scotland/Donmar Warehouse), Bondagers (Donmar Warehouse), Educating Agnes, Trumpets and Raspberries, All My Sons, Six Black Candles, The Breathing House, Victory, A View from the Bridge, The Taming of the Shrew, A Family Affair, The Marriage of Figaro (Royal Lyceum), Phaedre (Perth Theatre), Gilt, Road, Nae Problem (7:84), Viper's Opium, Earthquake Weather, Never-Before-

Seen Familiar (Starving Artists Theatre Company USA), Shooting Ducks, Just Frank (Theatre Royal, Stratford East), Swing Hammer Swing! (Citizens' Theatre) and The Government Inspector (Almeida). On television she has been seen in Dear Green Place, Taggart, Night and Day, Peak Practice, Big Cat, Looking After Jo Jo, The Macrame Man, Let Yourself Go and New Year Pieces. Film credits include The 39 Steps, The Pen, Karmic Mothers and The Priest and the Pirate.

Jessica Brettle *Designer*
Jessica completed a post-graduate diploma in Theatre Design at Bristol Old Vic Theatre School in 2005. Design work includes: The Government Inspector, Mish Gorecki Goes Missing, Perfect Analysis Given By A Parrot, Suddenly Last Summer, Defender of the Faith (Tron Theatre Company), Dracula (Firefly Youth Theatre), Falling/Flying (Hand Over Heart Theatre Company), Roadkill and Loves Times Beggar (Ankur Productions), Monaciello (Napoli Festival), The Lasses O', Ragged Lion (Rowan Tree), Can We Live Without You? (Lung Ha's), The Other, Martial Dance (Macrobert), The Glass Menagerie (Royal Lyceum), Black Watch (NTS), Aye Fond Kiss, Price Of A Fish Supper, Excuse My Dust (Oran Mor), Into The Woods, After Juliet, A Midsummer Night's Dream, The Chrysalids (Lyceum YT), City Madame, The Front Page, Krapp's Last Tape (Bristol Old Vic) and Fierce (Grid Iron).

Dave Shea *Lighting Designer*
Dave has worked in Scottish theatre for 16 years as a Lighting Designer, Production Manager and Technical Manager. He has designed lighting for Tron Theatre Company, 7:84 Theatre Company, Borderline, Suspect Culture, Complete Productions, Sounds of Progress, East Glasgow Youth Theatre, Tricky Hat Productions and Random Accomplice with whom he has worked on 8 productions. Previous design credits include The Littlest Christmas Tree, Mother Goose, Sleeping Beauty and Snow White of the Seven De'Wharffs (Macrobert), Little Rudi and Santa's Little Helpers (Tron Tall Tales). Recent design credits include Monaciello (Tron Theatre Company/Teatro Napoli Festivali), Bette/Cavett (Grant Smeaton Presents), Promises Promises (Random Accomplice), Little Johnny's Big Gay Wedding (Random Accomplice/National Theatre Scotland) and Smalltown (Random Accomplice).

Daniel Padden *Composer*
Daniel Padden is a musician and composer based in Glasgow. Recent theatre work includes Stars Over Kabul (National Youth Theatre), Curse Of The Demeter, Jason & The Argonauts (Visible Fictions), Horsehead (Faulty Optic). Recent short film/TV work includes Ever Here I Be (Kate Burton), Me & Her (Sarah Tripp), Half Life (Matt Hulse), 'Is It Just Me?', Black And White (Zam Salim). Daniel is a Music Practitioner with Paragon, working primarily in community and education projects. He is also a member of the bands Volcano The Bear and The One Ensemble.

TRON
THEATRE

The Tron Theatre is one of Scotland's leading building-based theatres set in the heart of Glasgow and housing a 230-seat main house, 50-seat studio, other small performance spaces, cafe, bar and places to meet. It is the home of Tron Theatre Company which stages a number of its own productions as well as co-productions and collaborations throughout the year, and plays host to a full programme of Scottish and international work from visiting companies.

Alongside all this work, the Tron provides space and opportunities to new and emergent artists to develop new work and experiment with theatre forms. The Tron also has a very busy education and participation programme which involves people of all ages and abilities in drama workshops, training, productions on our main stage, and work out in the community.

A highlight of the Tron year is Mayfesto, the now annual festival where live theatre is celebrated in an intensive season of in-house and visiting productions. As with all of the Tron's work, Mayfesto aims to use live theatre to stimulate discussion and engage audiences in an exchange of ideas.

The focus at the Tron is new work and contemporary classic theatre – theatre which speaks to the people of Glasgow and beyond about their lives now and theatre which presents new voices alongside internationally acclaimed writers, performers and artists. A Slow Air, premiered at Mayfesto 2011, is a perfect example of that philosophy and the Tron is proud to be associated with this fine new piece of writing.

Andy Arnold, *Artistic Director*

The Tron Theatre gratefully acknowledges support from

CREATIVE SCOT LAND
ALBA | CHRUTHACHAIL

Glasgow
CITY COUNCIL

New Arts Sponsorship
Grants Supported by the
Scottish Government In
conjunction with

Arts
&Business
Scotland

The Tron has the support of the Pearson Playwright's Scheme sponsored by Pearson PLC

The Tron Theatre is a Scottish Registered Charity SCO 12081

David Harrower
A Slow Air

faber and faber

First published in 2011
by Faber and Faber Limited
74–77 Great Russell Street
London WC1B 3DA

Typeset by Country Setting, Kingsdown, Kent CT14 8ES
Printed and bound by CPI Group (UK) Ltd, Croydon, CR0 4YY

A CIP record for this book
is available from the British Library

ISBN 978–0–571–28211–1

2 4 6 8 10 9 7 5 3 1

Characters

Morna
Athol

A SLOW AIR

Athol It was stuck through our letterbox, this note we got, the note that started it. Folded, half sticking out, like it had been left by one of the neighbours, y'know? We do things like that, look out for each other; families, couples, take post in, keep an eye out.

Change from when we moved here. God, how. Thought they were a load of stuck-up unfriendly b—s, y'know? What's it take to walk across the road and say hello or invite the new folk in for a glass of wine? I didn't even want to move to bloody Houston.

It was the sound of the planes overhead. Taking off, landing. I didn't sleep well for the first few weeks. So with that and the neighbours it was: what the hell have we done?

Remember saying to Evelyn, maybe they've smelt Edinburgh on me. Told her to expect flaming crosses on the lawn next, y'know?

But what brought us all together. 2007. The attack on Glasgow airport.

I was out walking with Clay that Saturday afternoon – Clay's our dog – and a front door opens and out comes Kenny and Kenny's wife, Mo. Of course they weren't Kenny and Mo to us then, just two afraid people. Had I heard the news? A car had been driven into the front doors, no one had been killed, they didn't think, but there was flames and chaos and
     Other neighbours came out their houses and wandered over. All of a sudden I'm at the centre of this crowd,

y'know, people are introducing themselves, patting the dog, bringing out cups of tea. I was surrounded.

Then that night we found out the bombers had lived in the village. The police cordoned off their house and there were the floodlights and TV cameras. The whole street, we just, we just seemed to fuse, y'know? As Evelyn said, out of the ashes.

I was here today. Neat, kind of spidery handwriting. *Been a long time. I wanted to talk to you but I guess not this time. See you.*

No name on the note. It was so
   Whoever left it, they'd got the wrong house. *I was here today?* I mean I was laughing, I was

I went through to my office – doubles as our lounge. I sit at the dining table there most nights, running my company into the ground. Suppliers to order from, payments to chase and chase, VAT returns, the never-ending search for new contracts.

I wanted to talk to you but I guess not this time.
   Evelyn was moving around in the kitchen next door and
   Came from nowhere. Mum and Dad's house years and years ago and my sister calling through to me about something. Morna.

What should we do about this?, Evelyn shouts through to me.
   Leave it, Evelyn, for God's sake.

We'd had a good day, been shopping, buying our food for the week. She walks ahead of me, picking stuff off the shelves. She knows what I like. We have this thing where every time we're shopping we put something in the trolley we've never tried before. So we'd gone from that, from being together and a jar of capers to this, the note and

8

I called the dog to come to me. I wanted to be outside, a long walk to the brae where the bench is.

We hadn't spoken one word to each other in fourteen years, me and Morna. Not a word.

Morna I was on the bus. This was the Wednesday morning. Was it? Aye. Still get the bus everywhere. Still stay in the same flat in Dalry. Still the same face, still the same arse. Aye, fasten your seatbelts, it's aw still still still wi me.

So the bus turns at the North British, sorry, the Balmoral, showin my age here, eh?, an down below I see my son, Joshua, right?, scalin the north side o the Waverley Steps wearin that long coat he wears, blowin up around him wi the wind. So I starts bangin on the window tae get him tae look up.

Doesnae hear me. Humphs left, along past the Waverley Centre. Was I deterred? I was not. I thump away again. Woman in front o me turns, tells me tae gie it a rest.

No, I will no, I goes, *that's my son down there. Keep your neb out o it, you.*

Bangin again. Louder. Right by her big fat heid.

Then get off the bloody bus, she turns an says.

I was almost thumpin her. But I wasnae goin tae get off cause I knew it wouldnae be arms open slow-motion wi a soft-piano soundtrack, ken?

We'd argued a fair bit of late. Never used tae. Slammin an swearin an screamin. Christ, you'd think we were married.

So we've left Joshua way behind an I'm busy givin this woman daggers. An then the bus stops, right?, in the traffic an Joshua goes an catches up wi us again, walks right alongside. An I see him an this woman sees him. Aw fuckit, I'm back on the glass again, bangin, an she's up on

9

her feet, *Driver, driver!*, aw that, face like fizz, then flies off downstairs. An we dae this aw the way along past the Mound. The bus'd pass him, he'd pass the bus. He walked wi his head down. Never noticed that before. I mean, he was about tae turn twenty-one, key tae the door. Head should've been up.

You have tae do somethin for your twenty-first, don't you? Well, you dinnae *have* tae but it's sad if you don't, eh? A waste.

I'm no doin anythin, he kept sayin. *No way. End of story.*

But it's no just about you, Joshua, I said tae him.

I should get tae celebrate, ken? A big thank you tae *me.*

I watched him walk right along towards Haymarket. Remember thinkin, good on you, son, walkin home, gettin the exercise. Because he, ken, an I've said this tae him, he could do wi a wee bit.

He stops at the crossing, waits for the green man. Sees it's a number 3, my bus, an his head lifts an he's back intae the upright homo-sapien position, ken? Clocks me finally. No wave. No smile. He shook his head. Just shook his head. Dinnae ken what the hell that meant. I got up tae get off, walk the last bit home wi him. Couldnae find the bugger.

Athol Evelyn was waiting for me when I got back. *Could it be Morna?*, she said.

Could be, I said as I walked past her.

But I wouldn't phone her, simple as that. Put my foot down. Might well have been stupid and childish. *Hated* her saying childish.

I went off to play golf that afternoon already wound up. Golf's not an escape for me like other men. I hate golf. This was business. This was Archie Swan. He's building the new estate out near Airdrie. Over a hundred houses means over a hundred tiled kitchens, bathrooms and en-suites, and that's five to six months steady work for my guys.

Known Archie since year dot. We served time together at Dodd's in Livingston. And somehow he's become what he is. House builder extraordinaire. Thousands of houses across central Scotland, whole estates, employing teams of men, sponsoring local f—ing fun runs, you name it.

I'd worked out a figure for him I was happy and confident with. Actually, so happy and confident I told him on the third green, I couldn't hold out. His considered reply?
Away and fuck off, Athol.

And off he pit-a-pats to the fourth tee.
The next few holes, silence. I'm trying to work out labour and costs and overheads on the back of my card, without hanging myself.
Green of the eleventh I give him my second quote.
Fuck's sake, Athol. Off he goes again.
Finally on the eighteenth, my final figure.
Athol, there's no way on God's earth you can do it for that.
He shakes my hand, congratulates me on my win.
I can make it work, I said.
No, he says, *I won't allow it.*
I won't allow it.

Archie I met that first day at Dodd's, didn't have a clue, didn't even know you used adhesive on tiles, y'know?
So how do they stay in place, dickhead?
That's how he got his nickname. Sticky.

So Sticky walked away from me again, just left me standing there. Strolled off towards the clubhouse. I bend down, pick up my ball.

Didn't even hit him. Hits his cart, bounces off it, rolls a bit. He's oblivious. But of course two members have to walk past at precisely that moment, pulling their trolleys. Couldn't even pretend it was a joke, y'know? Daft. My dad would've slapped me one.

I fled. I got home about half an hour later. Parked the car, pulled my clubs out the boot, turned and

Joshua. Morna's son.

Hey, Uncle Athol, do you remember me?

Pale round face. A few crooked teeth. Same green eyes. He'd written the note.

He was his mother as well. Still. God, so he was.

No one was home, he said.

His voice was quiet. Wouldn't look me in the eye. Only a faint trace of the boy. He'd made a leap I'd missed, through years I'd never see. The boy he'd been was so full of himself, so uncontainable, voice like water gushing.

I asked, *Why didn't you put your name on it?*

He pointed across the road. *Some Asian guy over there was watching me*, he said.

Aye, my neighbour.

He shrugged.

He puts his hand out, offering to take the golf clubs from me.

They were your grandad's, I said.

I took one of the woods out, gave it to him. He cradled it. His face.

I reached into the side pocket. Took out an old score card of Dad's that I keep in there. Inside it, a drawing of him, of Dad, done by Josh when he was wee, six or seven. Dad with his golf clubs. Found it in there after he died.

Aw man, he said.

You caught him, I said. *Definitely.*

He didn't have much time with Dad or Mum cause of

Well, cause Morna didn't want them to see him, simple as that.

Didn't know what I was supposed to do with him. I phoned Evelyn. The great mystery solved. Over the moon, she was.

Keep him there, she said. *Keep him there till I get back.*

You coming in then?, I said. And I warned him about the dog.

Another shrug and he follows me into the house.

Morna I went tae work the Wednesday afternoon as usual. I clean houses up in the Grange. Ken all the big poshies up there? Judges an advocates an surgeons, you name it. The *crème de la crème* o Edinburgh.

My favourite was Rosemary – Rosie. Her husband was Randolph. Rosie an Randolph. Beautiful sandstone house on Dick Place. Honest. And no content wi that, they also had a huge bloody flat in the New Town. Lyin empty. Cleaned that for them an aw.

That's one thing I'll say about my parents. Naming me Morna. You don't get too many Mornas. Mean that in a good way. They called my brother Athol which I always liked as well. Morna an Athol. A rare flash o poetry in their deadened hearts.

Rosie was good tae work for. *I think there may be too much to clean*, she says.

That's how she was wi me. Considerate. Always put her hand on my arm, forget she had it there. I think she was lonely. Adrift somehow, floatin around in this house, constantly rearrangin it. So skinny she was too. Nothin tae her. Never saw them in the same room aw the time I worked there. Always in different rooms. Seemed tae have lost interest in each other.

Remember once, Randolph was callin on her an we were both in the kitchen.

Rosie, he shouted. Then *Morna*. Then *Anyone*. Bellowin through the house. An she said tae me, *Pretend we're not here*. And we hid. In the food cupboard. He marched intae the kitchen, still shoutin then back out. She loved that.

If you'd told me at twenty I'd end up a cleaner, I'd have battered you.

I was a stupid cow. Everything I did was so as tae break away totally. Aw the family that came before me. Drivin buses, cuttin hair, pullin pints, polishin silver. Hard lives in black an white. Wi nae other choice. I see that now.

My grandmother's mother worked in the fields, for God's sake. Howkin tatties out near Dalkeith. Fuckin gettin up in the mornin tae stand at a hirin fair, her name called out by a factor. My grandfather who fought in the Second World War. The Gun Operations out at Craigiehall, near Kirkliston, served wi distinction. He saw the Luftwaffe flyin up the Forth. Heard the drone o them, up above him in the sky. I mean, who the fuck am I?

I see my mum an dad sittin on their sofa suite safe behind their double glazin. I cannae hear a sound. Nothin comes out, nothin goes in. Shh, Morna. Quiet. Be quiet.

So where was I? Digressin, eh? Fuckin Ronnie Corbett here.

Rosie's house. Polishin and hooverin and she's chattin away about a new paintin she's bought. An we got round tae talkin about our kids. I started talkin about Joshua tae her an how drawing was his thing. Drawing his comic books. He did a few drawings o me. Loads o me actually, cause, ken, perfection is hard tae capture.

He keeps tryin tae explain to me about the gutter. That's what they call the white space between the boxes o a comic. Where the artist decides what happens next. What tae draw in the next box. Anythin can happen in the gutter, he said.

Rosie smiles at me. *Your face lights up when you talk about him*, she says.

What?, I say. *Like I've been electrocuted or somethin?*

He'd stopped showin me his drawings. Cause I, I didn't get them. Or I said the wrong thing once, didn't take them seriously, I don't fuckin know.

It was on the bus goin back I decided. I was going to do somethin for him. He was going to get a twenty-first birthday party. Whether he fuckin liked it or no.

Athol Clay ran up to me like he always did when I opened the door.

Come in, I said.

Our last dog had bitten him once, years ago.

He didn't pat him or anything but didn't flinch either. Clay's a big Gordon setter, big elegant bruiser. They call them Black and Tans which you don't say out loud round here – rattle the ancestry, y'know?

The house is all on one level. Kitchen, utility room, lounge, bedroom, guest bed.

Aye, it's a bungalow. Death's waiting room. But it's surprised us. Or we've surprised ourselves.

He asked after Robert and Joanne to his credit. Aye, I liked that he asked. House has hardly any traces of them now. Noticed that showing him round. A photo in the lounge of us all on the top of Goat Fell one summer but that's about it. Used to have photos in my wallet when they were kids but seemed daft as they got older.

He was at college but said he never went.

Doing what?, I said. The shrug again.
Communications.

I offer him a cup of tea and he says, *You not got any beer?*
   Don't drink much at the best of times but we shared a
few cans.
   He's crouching down at my CD collection. Which,
alright, is alphabetical. He's pulling them out, groaning.
My pride taking a wee dunt, y'know?
   Jesus, he kept saying. *Aw, jeezo. Moan tae fuck.*
   He was from Edinburgh alright. Jeezo. Hadn't heard
that in a while. Moan tae fuck. *What's that strange
language you're speaking?*, I says.

He puts on the Simple Minds song, 'Don't You Forget
About Me'. The Minds as we called them. Love the song
now but then I thought they'd gone a bit
   But the early stuff. 'New Gold Dream', 'Promised You
a Miracle'. Dunna da da da da daaa.
   Bugger's laughing at me while I'm educating him. Up
on my feet, showing him how Big Jim Kerr used to move.
Jeezo, three cans in and I'm dipping, bending, in a floaty
white shirt.

He told me then what he was really into. I wasn't to laugh.
   No, I said, *I won't.* I wouldn't laugh.
   Cartoons, he said. Comic books.
   Blank. Last thing I was expecting to hear. *Kind of like
Marvel*, I said, *or kind of like The Broons?*
   And he laughed. Really laughed.

Evelyn's suddenly at the door. And Josh is up on his feet
and she's holding him, hugging him. I didn't know she'd
missed him so much. Took me back a bit. Like she'd kept
it to herself.
   She took a drink with us and I phoned out for a curry
and we stuffed ourselves. Och, the night just flew.
Suddenly it's past eleven and Evelyn says, *You can stay
the night if you want, Josh.*

That'd be great, he says.

When he was out the room, Evelyn looks at me and says, *Did you ask about Morna?*

Not yet, I said.

We were close for a few years. Course we'd slag each other and wish the other dead but there was a couple of years when we just seemed to

We found each other.

She'd lie on her bed and I'd be on the floor on some cushions and she'd put on a record and she'd read her magazine and I'd read mine and then we'd swap and spend more time reading each other's. Never my room she came to, too cool for that.

She left home in the middle of the night. None of us heard a thing. Age seventeen.

We took Clay out for his last walk, me and Josh. I always called him Josh. Never Joshua. Never liked the name Joshua.

We walked up to the brae. There was the faint rumble of a plane we couldn't see, just the ribbon of its vapour trail fading above us in the slow air. We stood there for a while.

I asked did he want to take the lead? I don't let Clay off the lead, he's not very obedient, he runs off, jumps up on people, it can scare them. He's a rescue dog from the Cat and Dog Home. We call him Clay – when we got him, his name was Claymore. What kind of eejits call a dog that?

We were heading back when he asks, *Did you ever see them? The bombers?*

I pointed to the house, over the fencing, six houses down, you can see the roof.

Saw them all the time, I said.

The doctor, Bilal was his name. He worked in the hospital in Paisley; locked up in jail now – the one smart enough *not* to douse himself in petrol – I told him I saw him in the Co-op a few times.

The one who died
   Kafeel Ahmed, Josh says, quick as a shot.
   He knew their names, where they were from, how they'd tried to bomb the nightclub in London the day before but the detonator hadn't gone off, how a holidaymaker at the airport had tried to save the burning Kafeel with a fire extinguisher. He knew his stuff alright.

So, Kafeel phoned me up about six months before they did it, I told him. He'd seen my van, he was thinking about a new floor for his kitchen, can I come round? So off I go, shirt and tie on, my measuring tape, book of samples, and I give him a quote. And we get chatting and I tell him about some contract work I'd been doing at the airport, top-end tiles for an executive lounge area. Told him about the security and the paperwork I needed to get my van in, all that and Kafeel's nodding away, listening to me prattle on.
   Josh's face
   So I'm to blame, I says to him. *It was all my fault.*

They were crap, he says. *Crap terrorists. Trust Scotland to produce such crap terrorists.*

Morna This better be good. This better be good. Joshua's new voicemail. Cheeky wee
   Left three messages for him, didn't hear a word back.

Wish he'd told me he wasnae comin home. There's a guy I kind of see. Drinks in my local. Always sits at a round table in the corner. Sir Galahad, I call him. Wouldn't say he was the love o my life but
   I like the go o him.
   He's a painter. No the Singin Butler kind. Walls an ceilings an that.
   An I ken he sees a few other women but

18

Wakin up wi him is way better for me than a bowl o Alpen.

I've no been too lucky wi the men. Soon as most o them saw Joshua hangin off me, it was a handbrake turn.
   Joshua's father. He was a weekend lost. He came, he went. Joshua kens who he is.

I didnae think I was ever goin tae have a bairn.
   See, faced wi that choice again.
   I dinnae ken.

I walked tae work, all the way tae the Grange. Through the Meadows which is aw students an suicide-joggers now.
   I always loved bein in Edinburgh even when I fuckin hated it. Never wanted tae leave even though there's times I should've. An if I had've, I would've come back, I know it.

I used tae bring Joshua up tae the old Odeon cinema on Clerk Street, tae the Saturday mornin kids' club there. Two hours to dae what I liked, free o him, poor wee sod. I'd walk around the shops then go an sit on a bench lookin up at Arthur's Seat, aw the English students walkin past gettin their free educations. I was SNP back then. Rabid SNP.

My dad would always say, pointin, *D'you see it, Morna?* Arthur's Seat – a proud lion restin on its haunches. *D'you see it?* My question back was always: *What's it got tae be proud o?*

Remember thousands o us marchin tae the Meadows, what year was it? '92. Hamish leadin us in 'Freedom Come All Ye'. Campbell Christie's big red fitba o a face. An aw, Willie McIlvanney, boomin intae his mike, *We're all mongrels in this nation.*
   I was near the front. *Who're you calling a mongrel?*, I shouted, *I'm a pure bred bitch.*

Fancied him rotten but he never took me up on it. His loss.

When I got tae Rosie's house, she wasnae in. Randolph opens the door. He was still a good-lookin man, even in his sixties. He made me a bit nervous, to be honest. Well, no that nervous. Kinda lifted the drudgery o the cleanin a wee bit.

He telt me first day no tae, under any circumstances, go intae his study. Like Bluebeard or somethin. But today it was, *Morna, where the hell are you?*

Shelves an shelves o books. A ladder on wheels tae reach them.
Close the door, he says, then tells me he's lookin for a rare book he's lost. His voice raspy, like escaped breath. Says he's feelin dizzy, will I go up an look for it? So I climb up an he's over at the bottom suddenly holdin it steady for me. No so dizzy now, Randolph, I'm thinkin. Only had old jeans on but they're tight an well my arse has always looked edible enough, ken?

So I'm stretchin up, lookin for this book. Then in my pinny pocket, my mobile rings. I ignore it but I look down at Randolph who's made this tuttin sound.
Sorry, I says.
He was at his desk now an he goes, he says: *What's the value? What's the value?*
I dinnae ken what he was on about. He put his head on the desk, rests on it. Then he just crumbled. A bloody stroke.

In the ambulance he's conscious now but ashen, face kind o twisted. Says tae me can I phone Rosie his wife? She'll put it right. I had already o course, but it was engaged.
Who's she talking to?, he said.
I dinnae ken, I'll keep tryin.
She'll put it right, he kept sayin. *She'll put it right.*

When I got her on the phone an told her, she howled. Howled. This woman who'd hid from him in the food cupboard. Never heard a sound like it.

I went tae the Dickens after. Sat there wi a g-an-t, congratulatin myself. No every day you save someone's life. Somethin to share wi Galahad.

Anyhow, I look at my phone, see who'd rung when I was up the ladder. Didnae recognise it. 01505? Where in hell's that? Who do I ken there? So I phoned it. It rings a few times, few times more.

Voice says *Hello?*
Who is this?, I said.
This is a phonebox, he says. *I was passing by.*
Where are you?
Houston, he says.
Houston?
Aye, he goes, *have you got a problem?*
I go, *What?*
Houston Renfrewshire no Houston Texas, he says.
Ha, ha, you're a funny guy. I hung up.

Houston's where Athol lives. I only ken that cause his wife, Evelyn, bothered tae tell me. Rang me up, sayin they were movin there. We dinnae talk any more, me an Athol. Good while now.

I like Evelyn though. Never goin tae be best pals, though, ken? She'd rung me a couple o times, a few years back. Her an Athol were havin marriage problems. She thought he was seeing another woman. Mum and Dad werenae long dead.

Maybe he's just gone mad, I said. I wasnae much help – how could I be? Dinnae ken what she expected.

But she wouldnae phone from a phonebox, I didnae think. Unless it was Athol? I'm sorry, Morna, forgive me, I was wrong, I love you etc. etc. Aye, right.

I phoned Evelyn at her work, see if it was her had phoned. Her soft voice the same.

A phonebox?, she said. *No, it wasn't me.*

Then: *Oh Morna. Did he not tell you?*

My heart stopped, ken? Silence.

He's here with us, she said. *Josh. He came yesterday and stayed the night.*

Right. Okay. Fine.

I have tae go, Evelyn. Should've added. *An his name's Joshua, for fuck's sake.*

But what I did say. *Do me a favour an keep him, will you?*

When he walked intae the pub Galahad's wi another woman. Bastard keeps me on my toes. Or is it my hind legs?

I went back tae the flat on my own. Didnae ken what tae do wi myself. Didnae like it, didnae like it one bit.

Athol In the morning Josh appeared in a Desperate Dan T-shirt and wouldn't stop going on about the mattress. Hands down, the best mattress he'd ever slept on. Could he buy it off us? The cheapest bloody IKEA.

Christ, what do you sleep on?, I says. *A bed of nails?*

I made him breakfast and he, och, he devoured it. Funny having someone that young in the house again. He said thank you and got up and washed all our dishes with too much washing-up liquid like Robert used to do. Bubbles everywhere.

What's wrong with the bloody dishwasher?

And then next thing, he's asking if we would, would we mind if, could he sort of hang out at the house for the day? Evelyn said yes, immediately. Not even looking at me. But *he* did. So, aye, all agreed.

But there was Clay. We both work during the day, so it was going to be Josh and Clay alone together. I didn't know who to be more worried about.

You've got my number, I said, *phone me if you have any problems.*

And what if I have any trouble with the dog?, he says.

In the van, before I left, I checked my mobile for the umpteenth time. There was a text from Archie Swan. Still deciding, it said. And aw, the relief. Start wondering what else I can do to sway him, y'know? Interflora?

Josh taps at the window, passes a book in to me. *Joe Sacco*, he said. *He's one of the best.*

Book was called *Safe Area Goražde*. The cover was a drawing of a UN convoy driving into a bombed-out village.

Don't call them comics, he said. *They're graphic novels.*

Driving back at the end of the day, I was, not worried but

Clay bounds up to me, big wolfy grin. Josh was sitting at the table, drinking a cup of tea.

You two get on?, I said.

Nothing to it.

Wasn't talking to you, I said.

There was a notebook full of drawings in front of him. He pushes it over. A drawing of our house. Delicate spindly lines. The old weavers' cottages. The mercat cross in the centre of the village. Looking down Four Windings. Some in pencil, some in ink. They were good.

It's my diary, he said.

He *drew* a diary. I thought that was pretty smart. Pretty unique.

I didn't recognise it at first. The airport bombers' house.

No law against it, he said.

And there wasn't, no, but people were still

Below it, there were more drawings. One was of Bilal the doctor loading a gas canister into a Jeep. Then a queue of holidaymakers waiting at checkout. Then Bilal in close-up, hunched over, his hands gripping the steering wheel.

They're not very good, he says. *Fanatics are hard to draw*.

Not as hard as Mohammed, I said. *Don't be going there.*

He asked if I had any photos of the family. I went and dug them out. Still in the old SupaSnap envelopes. Pictures he'd never seen.

We always

It was a thing my dad got us to do. We'd stand in a line and he'd say one, two, three, and we'd all have to jump as the photo was taken. Where he got the notion I don't know. It was such a non-him thing to do. Years of these photos of us in mid-air. An what started every time as a laugh, got

It wouldn't be right, we'd time it wrong so we'd be jumping six, seven, eight times. Again. Again. Jump. Jump. Everyone getting sick of it. Squabbling by the end. Laughing over.

We're passing the photos between us. He was looking at her, his mum, when she was a girl. Then Morna vanished from the photos.

Everything our parents did was wrong for her. They were small-minded. Stunted. Obsessed with scraping money together and holding on to it. They knew nothing about the world. Kept her shielded from it. Tried to smother her with their beliefs and values. Probably still thinks like that for all I know.

He asked about them. Mum and Dad. And

They came to their funerals but not in the family car. Sat at the back, beside the doors, the first ones out.

Basically, son, I said, *they were devastated. You never went and saw them. Never phoned them.*

He was taken aback. Face all

Eyes not meeting mine.

Did your mother forbid you? Eh? Could you not have made your own mind up?

The bloody shrug again. And he looked so

I left it.

We took Clay out again that night. Mr Rabbani was unloading shopping bags from the boot of his car. We said hello. His wife was there too with their wee girl, she pointed at Clay and shrieked and ran to hide behind her mum. We were all laughing. She did it every time she saw him.

Josh said, *Asians are scared of dogs.*

They were near enough to hear him.

They think they're unclean.

He bent down, stroked Clay. *How could they not like you, huh?*

We walked on a bit.

Then he said: *That's how they could stop suicide bombers. Stop extremism. Breed more dogs. Let them out on the streets. Let them roam free in airports and the underground. That'd sort it.*

Thought about this a lot, have you?, I says.

I had a pee, brushed my teeth before bed. He was outside the bathroom when I came out, the yellow light coating his face.

I need to ask uncomfortable things, he said.

Morna I woke wi Galahad beside me. He smiles in his sleep, I swear. I'd phoned him in the middle o the night, told him tae get his arse over here. He left first thing, didnae even stay for breakfast. Left my cup o tea sittin on the table. Had tae get out o there.

Longest guy I saw was

No the longest guy. Longest *time*. The longest time I saw
a guy was Richard. A musician, he was. And a chartered
accountant on the side. Four years I was wi him. I met
him on the train, comin back from a folk gig he'd been
playin in Linlithgow. Wee bit older than me wi a beard an
a pigtail down the back. The attraction wasnae immediate.

Me an Joshua would go wi him every week tae the Sunday
session in the Black Bitch in Linlithgow. Great name for
a pub, eh? We loved the Sunday afternoons there. *We're
off tae the Bitch!* Hamish Imlach, the McCalmans, Dick
Gaughan. The settled will o the Scottish people. An Nora
Devine, lovely Nora Devine who ran the folk club.

Richard adored me. Not sayin that tae big myself up.
Wanted tae marry me, become Josh's legal guardian,
move out tae East Lothian an raise Old Spot pigs. It was
just add water an stir wi Richard.

No man ever scared me as much. Showed me so much
o myself. Only time I reached for the safety rail. I'd do
aw that wi him now. Too late. I blew it.

Rosie was all *can't thank you enough, Morna, you're
wonderful, saved his life.* Aw that. Hugged an hugged
me. Randolph was still in the hospital but he was fine.

Course I still had tae do the cleanin. I'd saved his life
but the carpets still needed hooverin. She said no tae
bother but I wanted tae.

My cleanin rhythm was aw off. *Josh is with us. Josh is
with us.*

Athol would always called him Josh, never Joshua cause
I'd told him I'd named him after the U2 album. Athol was
Simple Minds tae the hilt. Worshipped them as much as
I did U2. I got intae folk music after but ken for a while
Bono, The Edge, Lypton Village, aw that stuff.

Athol'd call me a traitor. Aw the great Scottish rock music an you have tae go over the water? What great Scottish music? Fuckin Runrig? Great singalong band they were, every fuckin word in Gaelic.

End o my shift. Ask her, ask her. *Rosie, have you got a minute?*, I said an we sit down.

I told her about Joshua's twenty-first, howI really wanted tae do somethin for him. Could I borrow the New Town flat tae have the party in? Better than some fuckin house in Houston.

I was thinkin about the view over the private gardens an if it was warm we could go out there an sit on the grass.

An she looked at me. *How many?*, she said.

I dinnae ken exactly, I said. Then I went in low. *Four, five? Seven?*

She shook her head. I mind that. Before she spoke. *I can't, Morna, I'm sorry.*

Okay, I says. *Okay*. Thinkin, it's so little I'm askin.

You understand?

Yeah, I says.

An then, *It's not that kind of flat.*

I said somethin like, but it's no really a party it's just a few people, some drinks, nothin.

No, Morna, an up out her seat.

But Rosie –

Please, she said.

Took her a few steps before I realised. She was walkin out on me. She went intae the living room, closed the door behind her.

I got up, followed her. Knocked, opened the door.

Please, Rosie, I says. *It's only for a few hours. I'll pay. You can take it out o my wages.*

It has antiques in it, she said, *precious things.*

Like I'd never had anything.

Do I no clean this house every week? Do I no look after aw your precious things?

She was pointin at the door. All it did was make me go closer tae her.

Are you no always tellin me I'm the best fuckin cleaner you've ever had?

I turned, walked out. The long dark hall that took so bloody long tae clean wi aw the carvings an shit. An the neverendin dust an their shoes always just kicked off so I'd tae collect them back intae pairs.

I pulled my coat off the hook. The elaborate glass clock thing on the table an course my coat catches it an it smashes on the floor at my feet.

I mean, she'd got me so

She was walkin towards me, lookin at me an said I'd done it on purpose.

No, I didnae, I says.

You did. How could you?

Moan tae fuck. I just got out o there. Opened the front door; away.

Everything I fuckin did for her.

The fucking Grange, ken? Never been so pleased tae see Dalry in my life. Straight intae Dickens bar. Galahad there of course at his round table. A wee fumble in the bogs an before we know it, it's closin time an he's beggin tae come back wi me. So I let him.

Athol I wasn't needed into work until after lunch the next day. We took the dog out to Bridge of Weir for a walk along the old railway track there. Didn't talk much. After, I took him to the pub, treated him to his lunch. It was quiet. Just us and the torn-faced barmaid.

She's ill, he said.

I stared at him. He told me she'd had an operation on her

A lump on her neck.

How serious?, I said.

He shrugged. *You need a can-opener with her.*

You could've told me.

You could've asked, he said.

The food came, we started to eat. He asked me why we were like we were.

What's she told you?

I was always the one she could count on apparently. And then *even* I walked away from her. Stress on even. *Even* I. God, Morna, will you never change?

We drove back to the house. At the road-end he said to turn left, he wanted to see their house again.

I pulled up outside. It was just after two, an empty afternoon, no one around. The house is semi-detached, L-shaped, brick, pebble dash. Line of tall trees behind it.

That doctor worked in the hospital in Paisley for a whole year, I says. *Went to work every day and made people better.*

Must've really hated his job, Josh said.

He was up and outside the van suddenly, walking up to the front door. He steps to the side, presses his face against the window trying to see through the closed curtains. I got out, looking for faces at other windows, doors opening.

When I look back, he's started off around the side of the house. Christ. I walk round and he's at the back door, trying the handle. Forcing it up and down.

Josh.

I need to see inside, he said.

He kicks the door, bang. Shivers in its frame, a PVC white moulded thing, cheap. He kicked it again. Bashed his shoulder against it. It was a wee bit funny, him bouncing off this door.

Get out the way. I just booted it in. The door cracked open. No alarm.

There was nothing inside. Not a stick of furniture. And silent. Every socket taped off. Fridge dark and empty. The only living thing there was dust.

His eyes were wide, staring.
Give me your phone, he says. *Mine's out of juice.*

I looked at the floor I'd measured. Nine by fifteen. It was uneven, stained, the laminate ripped and torn. The police must've pulled it up. They'd lived in here, eaten in here, prayed in here.

I could hear Josh's voice in the next room. *Hey, Kafeel, you stupid burnt bastard, did you make it to heaven? Did you get your seventy-two virgins?*

The same three or four photos reprinted over and over. The Jeep exploding, the man on fire, the people running towards him. Their kitchen table littered with bomb-making equipment, switches, detonators, mobile phones.

Athol, he says. Holding up my phone. *I want a photo of you. Jump*, he says. *Jump. Moan, Athol.*
Dinnae be stupid.

I walked up the stairs. Into a room bright with light. Eyes blinking, adjusting. From the window, I could see our house; part of it.

I came back here, three more times. The third time the doctor opened the door. Did they want the new floor? Had they decided? He said sorry, there'd been a mistake, they'd changed their minds. I asked if they'd got a cheaper quote. Sorry, sir. I told him I'd lower mine, I'd do it for less, we could come to an agreement. Sorry, sir, he kept saying, no, thank you, thank you, sorry.

Did they laugh at me? Pity me? Letting me into their house to show their normality. A man who put on a shirt

and tie and rang their doorbell, samples under his arm.
No idea. Pathetic fucking stupid fucking

I threw up in the corner of the room. Bent over, my lunch
still warm in my stomach. Vomited all of it up and spat
and spat the yellow saliva from my mouth.

Josh was in the doorway. *You alright?* Staring at the sick.
Smiling.

I made straight for the van. Ignition key, engine revving,
van moving before he's even inside. *Shift your bloody arse!*

At dinner, his eyes were on me the whole time. I ignored
him; couldn't
    Evelyn asked us how our day had been.
    Alright, I says.
    And in the next moment, he says, *Athol threw up.*
    Evelyn frowning. *You were sick?*
    Aye, outside the pub. Something I ate.

Later, he said: *Are we taking Clay out?*
    Away and do it yourself, I says.
    Evelyn turned to me when he'd gone, asked me what's
going on. I shook my head, shrugged.
    Then I heard the shouting outside. And screaming. We
were both on our feet, front door, across the grass.
    Mrs Rabbani was cowering, holding her daughter,
shopping bags split at her feet. Kid bawling her head off.
Josh beside them.
    He knocked her over, she said.
    What?
    Her voice shrill, angry and pointing. *Your dog.*
    I ran into their house. Every light was on. Mr Rabbani
in the doorway.
    There, he said. Finger jabbing. He wouldn't go into his
own lounge.
    Clay, I said, *Clay?* He whined but I couldn't see him.

Please get your dog out of here. Points where a chair'd been pushed back. Clay caught behind it, stuck and wriggling, whining.

Get it out of my house, he said. *It is dirty. All this will have to be cleaned.* Hands circling around him. *All washed.*

I pulled the chair back and Clay came to me. I reached for the lead. There was no lead on him.

Get him out.

I took him by the collar. He peed on the carpet as I pulled him out, his whole body shivering, terrified.

I'll pay, I said.

Josh was on the street, the lead in his hand.

What did you do?

I thought he'd obey me, he said.

What did I fucking tell you? Are you fucking stupid?

The middle of the street, neighbours at their doors watching us. Kenny and Mo. Rhona. I pushed him.

Get in the house. He was the cause. Wanted them to see that. *Get in the house. Get in.*

Fuck off, he said and walked away from me along the street.

Who the fuck do you think you are?, he shouted.

I closed my eyes. Sitting on our bed. Evelyn beside me. She tells me to lie down and she lies down next to me and she puts her arms around me and holds me.

Morna Saturday, 6.30, the taxi drew up in the New Town an I get out wi two boxes o wine, a twelve pack o beer an a party-size bag o crisps under my arm. Still had the keys in my bag from when I cleaned it. I let myself in, closed the door behind me. Dinnae ken why I'm laughin. Desperate, eh?

Half an hour tae get the place lookin nice. Put aw her precious things intae the bedroom. Washed an dried some glasses. Beer in the fridge. Sidelamps on. Ready tae go.

I'd gone intae Joshua's room earlier, first drawer I open, bingo, his old phone. I sat down an texted every name on it. People I'd never heard of, never met, invited them all tae his party. Joshua last.

Seven o'clock came. And went. Seven-thirty. Had a glass o wine tae myself. Eight o'clock slid by. By eight-thirty, half the crisps were gone an I was slappin my hand away fae the wine box. Jesus Christ. I was startin tae take it personally. What's wrong wi my fuckin son, ya bastards?

I looked through one o his notebooks when I was in his room. There was some cartoon character called Crap Terrorist. Then loads o pages o naked girls wi numbered signs round their necks. I turned more pages. An old woman in a shawl pickin tatties, she's bent over starin at the ground cause one o the tatties is Joshua's face lookin up at her an smilin.

There was a long tube o paper held by an elastic band. It was a drawing, not cartoons, a real, a beautiful, careful drawing. The work he'd put intae it. Him sittin cross-legged, wi his head down. Two wee urns in front o him, full o ashes. A third urn, he was holding it, empty. On it, it said Mum. My wee head-down laddie.

I stood at the window lookin down ontae the street. All I could think o was the gutter.

No one was coming.

The gutter where anything could happen. An the next box. What happens in the next box.

A middle-aged woman standin in an empty flat, starin out the window. A woman on her own.

Fuck. There was a knock on the door. I jumped an

Fuck. A man an a woman in their sixties. Neighbours from upstairs. Saw the lights on, wantin tae ken if Rosie was there?

No, she's not, I says.

Who are you?, she says.

I'm Morna, her cleaner, before I remember I'm standin there all dolled up. I just slam the door on them.

An then *hheahhh*. The fuckin downstairs buzzer. I grab my coat an four seconds later I'm nashin down the stairs an out the close door past two laddies, Joshua's age, bottles clinkin in a plastic bag.

Where's the party?, one said.

Dicks!, I said.

I'm on Shandwick Place when I get a text. *I'm having a drink at the Black Bitch. Will you come? Joshua.*

I get on a train at Haymarket thinkin what is this, what the fuck is this? all the way tae Linlithgow Station, then I walk along the High Street past the old Ritz tae West Port an there it was in aw its glory. The Black Bitch. No a day different.

Richard told me the story. A black dog hundreds o years ago. Her master's in prison on an island in the middle o a nearby loch. Sentenced tae starve tae death but every day the dog swam out tae him wi food. Saved his life. Local people call themselves Black Bitches. After the dog's loyalty.

Place was stowed. Joshua was sittin on his own. There were things to be said but no then. No the night. I hugged him an kissed him an bought him a drink of course. An I gave him his card an I blew up a balloon an I made everyone around us sing Happy Birthday. An my camera, ken, just caught beautifully, Mum-why-the-hell-you-doing-this-tae-me?

    An there was a singer goin tae be singing later an
    Och it was just
    Crawlin from the wreckage, eh?

He went for a pee. I got talkin tae a few o the old guys there, playin dominoes, some o them remembered me.

One o them asked how Richard was. No idea, I says.
Then we had a laugh about the time I climbed up on the
bar tae dance an fell right over the other side.

An then he walked in. Unfuckinbelievable. Athol.

Athol The text I got said: *D'you fancy a pint? I'm
twenty-one today. I'll be in the Black Bitch in Linlithgow
from nine.*
    Nothing about what had happened. I umm-ed and
ah-ed a bit but, Evelyn

I parked the van at Linlithgow Station. I didn't know
where I was going, just headed along the High Street.
It was a warm evening. People were out walking. I took
a look at the Palace, never actually seen it in the flesh
before.
    The Black Bitch? Was she a strip-o-gram or something?

But no, sure enough, at the end of the High Street, this
old pub, the Black Bitch.
    There were a few auld fellas puffing away outside.
Dingy wee place with a lot of wood going on. Stone floor,
big stone slabs, cracked in places. They needed replacing.

Told myself I'd have a half. I never drink and drive but . . .
Just a half. For his birthday.

She was sitting in the corner. No sign of Josh. She was
pale. Like she'd faded. As gobsmacked as I was.
    She had a drink in front of her so I moved to the bar
to get my half but I ordered a pint.
    This was Josh. I knew instantly. I'd been set up.

Morna My own son. I felt like a stupid fuckin
    A fool.
    I got up and walked out o there headin tae the train
station, I didnae care.

I heard runnin behind me. Then Joshua pullin at my arm,
pullin hard.

What? What the fuck have you got tae say to me?

The street lights were on now an his face was half lit, half shadow, a black line for eyes like one o those villains in his comics.

Get back in there, he said. Fierce, ken? Pushes me. Puts his fuckin hand on me again an God help me, I swing at him.

He held his face, breath hissin wi the pain. Crosses the road, leans his back against the wall.

This is my night, he says.

An my heart just cracked, ken? Just fell open.

Athol When I turned back with my pint. Empty space, her drink still on the table. There'd been a free chair but someone'd taken it. Must've looked like a real lemon, standing there.

Some old fellas playing dominoes, a few watching a telly on the wall. A wee PA system with a guitar on a stand. I thought, at least there'll be some music.

I could just drink my pint and go. Drive back with the window down, take my time.

Then she was beside me. Right by my arm. You can *feel* blood. You can. Even after all that time. She looks at me. *You've put on the beef*, she says and sits back down.

Morna He stood like a statue in front of me, sippin his beer. Ridiculous. Nothin said for I dinnae ken how long. Fuckin ridiculous.

He looked a wee bit dull, to tell you the truth. Like he'd stopped surprisin himself.

You just goin tae stand there?

He shrugged, didnae move. Fuck's sake. I tap the guy opposite. *That chair you're on*, I says, *that was his.*

Aye well, it's mine now, he says.

I put my face closer. *He's my brother who I havenae seen in fourteen years. Let him have the fuckin chair. Please.*

He was softer around the face. Echoes o my dad in there.

Fuckin ambush, I said tae him.

He leans over, asks how I'm doin? His eyes searchin my face.

What's Joshua told you?

It's serious, he says. His voice wi flecks o Weegie runnin through it.

Well, it's no, I says. *They ken what they're doin at the hospital.*

Athol Whatever it was, was off limits. I wasn't going to get details like Josh never got details. Drop it.

What d'you make of Joshua then?, she said.

I told her he was nothing like I expected and Alarm bell goes off, red lights flashing.

What's that mean? What were you expecting?

He's great, I said. *It's been great to see him again. And his drawings, the cartoons.*

What, he showed you them?, she said.

Then: *He is great. Despite no help. Did it all on my own.* She said it twice. All on her own?

She'd done it with my mum and dad for years and after Joshua was born she moved on to me. Pleading, greeting, wanting money just for a few days, a couple of weeks. Something had always fallen through or she'd been let down by someone. Nothing ever her fault.

I lent you thousands. I said it straight out.

I was her personal cash machine for a few years. A soft touch.

And I paid you back.

Lost track what she still owed. Eight, nine thousand maybe?

Really, she says, surprised.

I took money out my business for her. That's illegal. I had to put it down as

Make things up, lie to the taxman.
Then

Morna It was stupid. A stupid, radge, mindless thing
tae do.

I was down to my last fiver. Drinkin like

Someone in the pub said tae try one o them nae-win-
nae-fee lawyers that were everywhere at the time.

Athol The dog went crazy, it wouldn't let go. I had to
stamp on the dog's back. Kick it.

Drove to the hospital like a madman, blood pouring
out Josh's arm. I've never been more distraught in my life.

Then a letter arrives from a lawyer, the Animal Scotland
Act, for pain and trauma caused.

My own sister tried to sue me.

I stopped contact after that.

Killed me doin it cause

Didn't think it'd be fourteen years.

Morna The singer started singing an playing her guitar.
She looked about sixteen years old.

Remember he had to stay the night wi Joshua once. I was,
I was stuck somewhere an

He left his work an picked Joshua up from school an
made him his dinner an watched TV wi him, put him tae
bed an slept on the couch till the mornin. Always be
grateful tae him for that.

Tae do aw that an then

Wouldnae pick up the phone or answer the door.
Joshua askin me for months what's happened tae Uncle
Athol an Auntie Evelyn?

I was just left tae myself. Cut adrift by own family.
None o them gave a flyin fuck.

This great old folk pub, what's she gie us? Fuckin Del A-
fuckin-mitri. Nothing ever happens. Athol fuckin tappin
his foot.

He goes intae his pocket, unfolds a piece o paper, slides it quietly over tae me. A bank statement in Joshua's name. Total amount, twenty-one thousand pounds.

Athol For his twenty-first. Mum and Dad and me set it up for him. She stares and stares at it.

I wasn't to be told?, she says. *I cannae be trusted. His mother.*

I held out my hand, wanting it back but she kept on.

We can't trust Morna, can't trust Morna.

People turning their heads, looking at us.

Just as well it's for him then, I says, *not you.*

He's not getting this, she says.

Morna I was boilin mad. My fuckin

You an them. All o you.

He reaches over, tries tae take the paper from me but I pull it away an scrunch it up an throw it across the room

You can go fuck yourself.

Excuse me. There's a loud voice talking above me. *Hey, excuse me.*

An old guy pulls my sleeve, pointing at the singer.

D'you mind being quiet? I'm trying to sing here.

I fix her wi a look. *Aye, I would, hen, if it was fuckin worth hearing.*

Athol Aw Jesus. Intake of breath all round the room. Two old blokes starts chanting *Fight, fight.*

The girl says, *Frank. Can you get these two out of here?*

Morna's on her feet. *Dinnae worry.* Turns at the door. *D'you no ken any real songs?*

And she's gone and course I'm the one gets the dagger look from the young lassie, like I'm the bloody boyfriend or something an I say, God knows why, *She's my sister.*

I get up and walk out as well, after I've scrabbled about looking for the statement.

Outside, she lights up a fag she's bummed off someone and we just stand there, no saying a word.

Morna When they died Athol got left the house an a big whack o money an I got next tae nothin. Thought that was their final say, but naw, this, the bank statement, this was Athol an their's last word, last judgement on my life, the way I've lived my life.

He stood beside me in his fleece an jeans. Just let me stand there, no even attemptin

Both our mobiles go off at the same time.
I'm in the lounge bar when you're done. Joshua.

Athol I was expecting him to be in there on his own but no, he's with a couple of mates, they're laughing and joking, a stack of empty glasses on the table in front of them. A lad called Craig on one side and a girl, a young woman, I should say, on the other. Obviously his girlfriend, how close she was sitting to him.

He looks at us both. Tells Morna to sit down and I was to buy him his birthday drink.

Morna Rachel was her name. Been seein each other eight months.
The night o a thousand surprises, I said.
Josh gives me a warning look.
I shook her hand.
Finally we meet, she says. An then: *You've got a lot of parties on the night.*
That was a wee bit sly, I thought. Aye, a wee bit. First thing tae say tae me.
Aye, she was quite pretty, I suppose. She was all over him, almost sittin in his lap. His hand strokin her arm so gently you'd hardly notice it.
There was a graze on his cheek which didnae make me feel great, have tae say.

40

Athol I got them all drinks and got myself a half and sat down beside Rachel. Soon as I did it, I'm thinking should I have sat next to Morna?

His mate clunks five shots down on the table. One's pushed over to me. I shook my head, no. It'd mean the train home and then coming all the way back for the van.

I could see Morna looking at me. Knew exactly what she was thinking. I lick the salt and tip my glass back then bit the lime.
   Nastrovya, I says. Nastrovya?

Three pints I had after that. And two more shots. And a whisky. Unheard of.
   This's going in the diary, Uncle Athol. A drawing of you, drunk.
   I lean over and ask Rachel if she knew her boyfriend had been named after an overrated U2 album. No reaction.
   His middle name's Tree, I say.
   Ignore him, Rachel, Morna says. *He went to school in a special bus.*

The booze was coursing through me. And more people were piling in the later it got to closing. And then Morna spots the singer and goes crashing over to her and buys her a drink and suddenly she's at our table with her guitar and she's singing for us all.

Morna Course he had tae ask her if she knew any Simple Minds. *Who?*, she said. She sang an old folk song for Joshua. A beautiful slow air. Cannae mind the name o it. Whole room went quiet.

My mother, ken, phoned me when I was pregnant wi Joshua. It was late at night, her voice hushed. I kind o imagined she'd driven tae a phonebox on a quiet country road, ken?

Morna, it's your mother. Who else would whisper like that? *Me and Dad have had a talk. We're willing to pay for you to terminate.*

She put my dad on: *Morna, your mum's finding this very hard.*

That was my

I brought Joshua up wi every bit, every piece o me. And I know I fucked it up at times but look at him. That's my beautiful boy.

Never told Athol about that phone call. He doesnae need tae know.

Athol I was watching Morna, her eyes fixed on Josh and Rachel. She looks at me. I look at her. She smiles. I see the pain and the fear. And I know. And she knows.

Morna Then everyone was dancin. We were aw up on the seats an the tables, the whole place. Like the old days, almost. Athol didnae dance, thank God, sat watchin everyone.

I did too, to be honest. My days dancin on tables are gone.

Athol Later, we're squeezed in beside each other and she's taking the piss out of me, how come I've gone all Weegie? Then my phone goes and I see his name come up

I've got it, I've got the bloody job.

Archie!, I says

A fucking golf ball!, he says, raging. *You threw a fucking golf ball. It's all round the clubhouse. A big fucking joke. You just blew it, Athol.*

Listen, Archie, I says, *please*, and then I see Morna looking at me and

A million years ago in Edinburgh. Preservation Hall. Me and Archie, two apprentices out on the lash and in come Morna and her pals.

Morna I took the phone off Athol.

Sticky? Is that you, ya fuckin heartbreaker?

Who is this?, he says.

Morna.

Fucking hell.

What happened, Sticky?, I says. *You never fuckin phoned me back.*

It was thirty years ago, Morna. No one calls me Sticky now.

You married now, Sticky?

Aye, I am.

You happy, Sticky? Cause you're makin my brother look awfy miserable.

He always looks awfy miserable, Morna.

Remember you left me wi a smile, Sticky.

Aye. Take care, Morna.

You too, Sticky.

An tell Athol I'll call him tomorrow.

Walkin tae the station for the last train, Athol's round me, am I sure that's what he said? He'd phone me tomorrow?

Aye, Athol, gie's peace, will you, fuck's sake.

Remembered how fuckin annoyin he could be. Buzzin in your face.

Josh an the girlfriend were up ahead o us. I asked him about Evelyn. Maybe it was the drink inside him.

Athol I'd been seeing someone in Glasgow. Not for long. And I finished it.

Evelyn never knew about her. We hadn't been getting on well. Moving to Houston was an attempt to mend it. But the neighbours not talking to us and the constant sound of the planes, I came to hate the house, the village. Nothing was right.

I phoned the woman. I wanted to see her again. She said yes.

I told Evelyn I was having a drink with Archie that night.
Fine.

That was the day of the airport bombing. Before I left,
I took Clay out for a walk and Kenny and Mo opened
their door and walked towards me and then the other
neighbours one by one until I was surrounded.
   I never saw her again.

Morna He said Evelyn never knew an
   I had tae tell him he was wrong, she did know. She'd
guessed.
   He stopped walkin. Stood there in the middle o the
pavement. Said he just wanted a minute. But I stayed
there wi him.

When we got tae the station, he had tae go through the
underpass for the Glasgow platform. He took Joshua
aside and said something to him. He ruffled his hair and
gave him a big hug. And then we had a quick hug, so
it was

When we get on tae our platform he's already standin
opposite, talkin on the phone tae Evelyn, askin her tae
come and pick him up. The track's so narrow the
platforms are nearly touching there.
   Give her my love, I says.
   He came off the phone, stood there, looking back over
at us. Looked at me.
   Didnae ken where tae look suddenly. Him neither by
the look o it. It was kind o awkward. He held up his
mobile.
   I'll call you, he says over the track.
   I willnae hold my breath then, I said back.

He'd given me the bank statement. You give it to him, he
said. Say it's from all of us. You, me, Mum and Dad.

Athol I was looking at the photos Josh had taken on my phone. Empty kitchen, empty lounge, empty bedroom. That dead, empty house. I pressed delete. Delete. Delete.

Then I heard her singing.

Morna sings part of '(Don't You) Forget About Me', as sung by Simple Minds.

I could see my train way up the track coming towards me.

And then Josh's voice telling us, quick, quick, he wants a photo of the two of us.

Morna And he tells me tae stand on the edge o the platform.

Athol And I've to stand on the edge of my platform to get us both in.

Morna And he crouches down, holding his phone out and

Athol One, two, three, he says.

Morna One, two, three

End.